A FOUNDATION FOR A GOOD MANAGEMENT – 2012

-Shops in England-

J. Polenceus

Many thanks to the Management Consultancies Association
and Business Link in England

CONTENTS

FOREWORD

We are inundated with a big amount of information. There is plenty of world-class Business advice out there-but where is it? Our Finance Information Sources is a highly selective and well-researched collection of sources.

Fortunately, many management fundamentals have remained unchanged. Through 20 years working with private companies I have learned what works and what does not. Trough this guide, it is my aim to help business to understand the laws that affect you are an important part of running a successful business.

Retail is the UK's largest employment sector. Comprising nearly 300,000 ext remely diverse businesses from the largest chains to the smallest one-man ba nds, it employs around three million people – a tenth of the workforce – selli ng everything from clothes and white goods to food, books and toys. It gene rates sales of £265 billion, a third of UK consumer spending. Moreover, it u nderpins the UK's massive tourism, leisure and hospitality industries.

The sector has had 14 years' steady growth and in the summer 2008 there were 100 retail-led developments across Britain, including 20 new shopping centers. The sector expects to create 250,000 new jobs by 2014. Yet unless the challenges being faced by this economic colossus are tackled imminently and comprehensively, they pose a serious threat to its growth, future profitability and economic contribution.

This guide will help you decide whether is good for you. It shows how you can find the right shop, and highlights the key issues you need to consider.

CHAPTER ONE

SETTING A SHOP IN ENGLAND

Introduction

Setting up a shop in England should be an exciting process but in fairness it is a crucial decision to consider. Managing people, selling to the public and having the necessary dedication are common requirements of different types of shops.

Without the right advice it can also be a minefield where legal matters are concerned. Too often it is not until matters reach crisis point that people ask for a solicitor's help. But by then, if a solution is available, it is much more costly than taking simple action that could have prevented the problem in the first place. Spotting trouble before it comes is better than cure. This guide can help to giving advice on all the typical problems that a new shop can face and take steps to prevent them.

1 Assess yourself

You must be prepared to sell and you will need entrepreneurial flair. Any advice or degree would give you a business blueprint - but it won't automatically give you customers.

You'll need to be well organized and enjoy building relationships working in partnership to continue growth. You'll need to work hard, probably for long hours. Do you have the necessary dedication? Running your own business can be stressful. Think how you react to pressure. You may be starting up in business because you want to be your own boss. Do you like office work?

Or would you prefer a business that involves physical labor or using a particular skill? Are you happy working on your own? Or would you be good at recruiting, training and managing employees? Do you like dealing with members of the public? Or would you prefer a shop where you sell to business customers? Are you weak in particular business skills such as finance? This guide offers the support you need in those areas.

1.2 Business structure

The structure of a business is vital to its success. It is important to give it careful consideration because it can affect things such as the tax and National Insurance contributions to pay, pension payments, the records and accounts to keep and the way management decisions are made. There is a say that you would like to keep in mind when organising your business: 'fail to prepare- prepare to fail'.

Under English legislation, there are essentially three fundamental forms by which a business can be conducted: as sole trader, a partnership or as a limited company.

1.2.1 Sole trader

Sole trader is the simplest way to run a business. A sole trader is an individual who is conducting the business in her/his own name, keeping accounts and any profits, but she/he is also personally liable for any debts. If a sole trade incurs debts the creditors can seek legal redress against the sole trader as a private individual.

To run a business as a sole trader the owner has to register first as a self-employed for Income Tax and National Insurance (NI) purposes with Her

Majesty Revenue & Customs (HMRC), www.hmrc.gov.uk, Self-Employed Helpline 0845 915 4515

Your National Insurance Number (NI)- In order to register you will need your NI number. If you don't have one, please call Jobcentre Plus on Tel 0845 6000 643.   You will need to attend an 'evidence of identity' interview at a Jobcentre Plus or   Social Security office.

When to register?. You should tell HMRC as soon as you start working for y ourself - you can't register in advance. If you delay registering more that thre e months, You may be fined £100 if you fail to register within three months of becoming self-employed. There is no fee for registration. You will have to pay further penalties if payments become due and have not been met.

Information you will need to provide; make sure you have all of this to   h and if registering online as you cannot save the details and return at a later da te once you start to complete the online form.

- Name
- Address
- National Insurance Number
- Date of birth
- Contact telephone number
- Contact email address
- The date your self-employment commenced
- The nature of your business
- Your business address
- Your business telephone number
- Your Unique Tax Reference (UTR),if you were previously within Self Assessment
- The business's UTR - if you are joining an existing partnership
- Where relevant, the full name(s) and date(s) of birth of your business partner(s)

1.2.2 Partnership

Partnership applies when two or more people share the profits, risks, loses and responsibilities of running the business, which means an equal share of any profits but also personal liability for any of the partnership's debts. If one particular partner cannot meet her/his own share of the losses, then the other remaining partners may become liable for the defaulting partner's share of the debts.

If you are in a partnership, each of the partners must register separately as a self-emplyed.

Information concerning a sole trader's and partnerships accounts will remain totally confidential to the business's owners and the taxation authorities.

1.2.3 Limited Company

In the UK it is a very common method of conducting a business. If the company cannot pay its debts, the principle of incorporation, the shareholders (investors) cannot be held personally responsible for their business's debts and liabilities.

If a company cannot meet its liabilities (responsibilities) then the maximum amount a shareholder can lose is the amount of their original investment in the firm's share capital. The accounts of a limited company will be open to public inspection and close examination.

1.2.4 Public Limited Companies

A number of limited companies are designated as *public limited companies,* and show the designation of plc. A public limited company may have massive numbers of comprising of individuals shareholders and financial institutions.

A company that is designated as a public limited company must have at least a minimum issued share capital of £50,000. The company's Memorandum of Association must also specify that it is a public limited company and the company must have at least 25 per cent of its share capital paid-up (Companies Act 1985, sec 1, 11 and 25).The ability to offer shares on the stock market makes it easier to raise capital;

Any limited company that is not designated plc is deemed to be a private co mpany.

1.2.5 Private Limited Companies

Private limited companies can be limited by shares or guarantee.

private limited company usually it is owned privately by a small group, such as a family and they may often be actively involved in the management of the company. They are not allowed to offer shares to the public and can operate through just one director.

A private limited company cannot trade its shares on the stock market. Although private limited companies are usually small in size, they are expensive to set up and have to produce proper accounts. Furthermore, unlike a sole trader, private limited companies have to pay auditors, hold meetings as stipulated in the Companies Act and share profits between all of the shareholders.

In British and Irish law, a *private company limited by guarantee* is an alternative type of business structure used primarily for non-profit organizations as charities, that require legal personality.

A guarantee company does not usually have a share capital or shareholders but instead has members who act as guarantors. The guarantors give an undertaking to contribute a nominal amount (typically very small) in the event of the winding up of the company. It is often believed that it cannot distribute its profits to its members but (depending on the provisions of the articles) this is not actually true.

However, a company limited by guarantee that distributes its profits to members would not be eligible for charitable status.

Under the british law *a private company limited by shares,* usually called a private l imited company (Ltd) has shareholders with llimited liability and its shares may not be offered to the general public.

'Limited by shares' means that the company has shareholders, and that the liability of the shareholders to creditors of the company is limited to the capital originally invested. A shareholder's personal capital is thereby protected in the event of the company's insolvency, but money invested in the company will be lost.

To register your business as a limited company you have to contact the Companies and House;

PO BOX 29019
21 Bloomsbury Street
London
WC1B 3XD
Website: www.companieshouse.gov.uk
E-mail enquiries@companies-house.gov.uk
Tel: +44 (0)303 1234 500 (national call rate)
Minicom No. 029 2038 1245

Other company formats include franchises, social enterprises and co-operatives, see chapter two

1.3 Commercial Properties

The human nature of shopping has not changed so much despite the fast paced development of the e-commerce or online shopping. People still like to feel in control of the situation and according to their own preferences, getting the right information at the right time on the journey – form initial attention grabbing through to desire and rational decision-making.

A good achievement or failure of the shop depends in many cases where it is situated, its building facilities, its financial strength and trade ability, the competence of its equipment, the protection of new products, titles or designs afforded by patents, the efficiency of its sales departments, and finally to be better organized than its competitors.

When choosing premises for your business, it is important that you fully understand the terms of the lease. Can the landlord increase the rent? If so, by how much? Will you find yourself paying ever-increasing service charges? Will you need planning permission for a change of use?

1.4 Council Tax Valuation

The Valuation Office Agency (VOA) offers a searchable list of business rates valuations - allowing you to check the 2010 and 2005 rateable value for your property.

You will be able to;

- Find your property valuation
- Compare your valuation with others

- Amend your property details
- Appeal your valuation or find your appeal information

If you are a Rating Agent, the application offers an Agent mode with extra search options.

For further information on business rates and advice on using the rating list application, call the VOA Helpline on Tel 0845 602 1507

1.5 Industrial planning

The topic covers floor space, rateable value, and rateable value per square metre for different types of commercial and industrial properties in England and Wales; property and employee statistics for town centres and retail cores; and the extent of retail development in England.

1.5.1 The planning system

The planning system helps to ensure that development takes place in the public interest, in economically, socially and environmentally sustainable ways. It has a major impact on how local neighborhoods look, feel and function. It also has a role to play in helping to cut carbon emissions, protect the natural environment and deliver energy security.

1.5.2 Background

The core elements of the planning system are development plan making and development management. These activities are primarily undertaken at the local level.

Local planning authorities prepare development plans, through consultation with local communities, which set the broad framework for acceptable development in their area.

Authorities are also responsible for development management. This includes statutory requirements on publicising, consulting on, and determining most applications for planning permission, taking into account the opinions of local people and others. They also operate allied discretionary services including pre-application advice to prospective developers and enforcement against breaches of planning legislation.

The Department for Communities and Local Government supports plan making and development management, principally through the provision of planning legislation, national planning policy, and guidance.

The Secretary of State has the power to 'call in' planning applications for determination rather than letting the local authority decide (for example, if they conflict with national policies on important matters). Planning appeals can be 'recovered' for decision by Ministers, for similar reasons.

1.6 Opening hours

Typical opening times are;

Mondays to Saturdays - Small shops normally stay open 9am to 5:30pm, (10am to 4pm), (7am to 7pm,) (or 11am to 5pm). Some shopping centres stay open until 8 pm or later. Large supermarkets are open for 24 hours except for Sundays. Many supermarkets, superstores, and groceries otherwise open from 8am until 10pm from

Public Holidays / Bank Holidays Shop opening times 10am to 4pm (or 11am to 5pm). On public holidays, some shops open and some shops do not. As a rule banks will be closed, most supermarkets and large stores will be open although with reduced Sunday opening hours, and in larger towns many shops will open.

Christmas Day (Trading) Act 2004 regulates opening hours of large shops on Sundays and Christmas Day. The Sunday Trading Act also prohibits large shops from opening on Easter Sunday. Over the Christmas and New Year period, all shops are closed on Christmas Day (December 25) and a some shops are closed on New Year's Day (January 1). However, an increasing number of shops are now opening on Boxing Day (December 26), which is when many start their 'New Year' sales.

Easter It is likely that most shopping centers will be closed on Easter Sunday and there will be reduced shopping hours on Easter Monday (often from either 10 or 11 o'clock in the morning).

In Villages Some rural shops still follow the tradition of an early closing day (usually a Wednesday) when the shops close at 1.00pm.

Banking Hours The major high street banks in England and Wales are Lloyds, Barclays, Midland and National Westminster (Nat West). In Scotland, they are the Bank of Scotland, the Royal Bank of Scotland and the Clydesdale Bank. Generally Monday-Friday 9:30 am-3:30 pm. Some branches stay open until 5:30 pm, and a few are open Saturday morning from 9am till 12noon. Most banks will have an ATM (Automated Teller Machine) outside the bank where you can draw out money with a credit or cash card. Many of these are available to use 24 hours a day, but some do still close for a few hours during the night.

Sundays Trading Sunday shopping has become popular in recent years and most large shops in towns are open for business. Shops are only allowed to trade for 6 hours on Sundays. Sunday trading rules came into force in

1994 which allowed shops in England and Wales to open legally on a Sunday. As a result, some shops that open on a Sunday face restrictions on their hours of trading.

Currently, small shops with a floor area of up to 280 square metres (3,014 square feet) can choose their own Sunday opening hours. But employers must be aware that staff who work on a Sunday may have special employment rights.

Many large shops with a floor area greater than this limit can only open for a set number of hours on a Sunday. Some categories of large shop are exempt from the restrictions placed on opening hours by the Sunday Trading Act 1994.

They are;

- Shops such as off-licences that sell only or mainly alcohol
- Shops in airports and railway stations
- Shops at service stations
- Registered pharmacies that don't sell any goods other than medicinal
- Products and medical and surgical appliances
- Shops on a farm that mainly sell their own produce
- Shops that wholly or mainly sell motor or bicycle supplies and accessories
- Shops that only supply goods to aircraft or sea-going vessels on arrival at, or   departure from, a port, harbour or airport exhibition stands selling goods

Remember that your employees may still have special employment rights if they're required to work in your shop on Sundays.

1.7 Main Department Stores in England

Marks & Spencer - for cloths and food
Debenhams - for cloths
John Lewis - for fashion, toys, homewares, electrical, and gifts
British Home Stores - for clothes and household items Boots -for toiletries
Superdrugs- for health, beauty, fragrances, toiletries as well as health advice
WHSmith - for newsagents, stationers, Cds and DVDs, books
Woolworths - for toys, entertainment, kids clothing
Argos House - toys, entertainment, furniture, electrical, gifts, stationery
Fraser Liberty's- for cloths, accessories, beauty, gifts, fabric, stationery
Harrod's - for grand pianos, toys, entertainment, furniture, electrical, gifts, stationery, food, cloths, accessories, beauty, Cds and DVDs, books
Selfridges - for toys, entertainment, furniture, electrical, gifts, stationery, cloths, accessories, beauty,
Currys -for electricals
PC World - for computer and phone devices
HMV- Cds and DVDs, books
Carphone Warhouse - for mobiles and broadband devices

Main Supermarkets are;
Tesco (Britain's largest supermarket chain)
Asda stores ltd supermarkets
Iceland
J Sainsbury
Somerfield Waitrose
Morrison's

Charity shops and sales of goods

Although the sale of donated or bought-in goods by a charity or its trading subsidiary is a business activity, the exact VAT treatment of your supplies depends on both the circumstances of the sale and the nature of the goods:

- if the goods are donated your supplies will be zero-rated, subject to some conditions - however, this may not apply if you make use of the goods before selling them, or have a prior arrangement with the donor relating to the sale of those goods

- if your charity buys goods to sell on, your supplies will normally be standard-rated (unless the goods are zero-rated by law, for example children's clothes, books, etc)
- if bought-in goods are being sold at a fundraising event, they may be exempt from VAT -

The Main Charities Shops in England are;

Human Relief Foundation
Sir William Crookes
Salvation Army
Oxfam
British Association of Cancer
Cats Home

1.8. Apply for Licenses

- Alcoholic drink retail (includes off-licenses)
- Musical instrument retail and repair (includes instrument parts and accessories)
- Meat, poultry and game retail (includes butchers)

- Audio-visual equipment repair (includes conferencing systems)
- Furniture retail (includes related articles such as window blinds, mattresses and fixtures)
- Beauty and toilet products retail (includes sun tan preparations)
- Take-away food shops (includes outlets providing food for delivery)
- Children's clothing and baby goods retail (also select leather products retail if applicable)
- Audio-visual equipment retail (includes conferencing systems and consumer electronics)
- Sports equipment retail (also select clothing, footwear, guns and ammunition wholesale if applicable)

To apply visit the web; www.businesslink.gov.uk

CHAPTER TWO

CO-OPERATIVES, FRANCHISES AND SOCIAL ENTERPRISES

Introduction

Some company formats include co-operatives, franchises and social enterprises . It is a good idea to take legal advice and carry out careful research before choosing the legal status of your business.

There are many other times when taking legal advice might be useful, including when buying and renting business premises, taking steps to protect your intellectual property and when buying a franchise.

2.1 Co-operatives

A cooperative (also co-operative or co-op) is a business organization owned and operated by a group of individuals for their mutual benefit.

A cooperative is defined by the International Cooperative Alliance's Statement on the Cooperative identity as 'an autonomous association of persons united voluntarily to meet their common economic, social, and cultural needs and aspirations through jointly owned and democratically controlled enterprise'.

A cooperative may also be defined as a business owned and controlled equally by the people who use its services or by the people who work there. Various aspects regarding cooperative enterprise are the focus of study in the field of cooperative economics.

2.2 Buying a Franchise

Buying a ready-made business is an appealing option, but what about any previous liabilities that may come with it or the small print in the sale agreement? All too often, people find themselves trapped in a deal with expensive products and no support from the franchiser. What if the franchise doesn't come up to expectations? Can you get your money back? Your solicitor can give you advice on all the common problems associated with running a franchise.

Taking on a franchise is an option worth considering for anyone who wants to run a business but doesn't have a specific business idea or prefers the security provided by an established concept.

The right franchise can give you a head start. Instead of setting up a business from scratch, you use a proven business idea. Typically, you trade under the brand name of the business offering you the franchise, and they give you help and support.

Successful franchises have a much lower failure rate than completely new businesses. However, you will still need to work hard to make the franchise a success and you may have to sacrifice some of your own business ideas to fit in with the franchisor's terms.

A true business format franchise occurs when the owner of a business (the franchisor) grants a licence to another person or business (the franchisee) to use their business idea - often in a specific geographical area.

The franchisee sells the franchisor's product or services, trades under the franchisor's trademark or trade name, and benefits from the franchisor's help and support. In return, the franchisee usually pays an initial fee to the franchisor and then a percentage of the sales revenue.

The franchisee owns the outlet they run. However, the franchisor keeps control over how products are marketed and sold and how their business idea is used.

2.2.1 Distributorship and dealership

You sell the product but don't usually trade under the franchise name. You have more freedom over how you run the business.

Agency - you sell goods or services on behalf of the supplier.

Licensee - you have a license giving you the right to make and sell the licensor's product. There are usually no extra restrictions on how you run your business. Some businesses offer franchises that are multi-level marketing.

Self-employed distributors sell goods on a manufacturer's behalf. You get commission on any sales you make, and on sales made by other distributors you recruit.

Be aware that some multi-level marketing schemes may be dishonest or illegal.

2.2.2 Franchise Agreements

When you franchise your business, you - the franchisor - enter into a legal agreement with the franchisee. A clear, written contract is essential.

This franchise agreement sets out what rights and obligations you each have. Key issues include what territory the franchisee can operate in and whether they have exclusive rights in that territory what rights the franchisee has to use your intellectual property - eg your trademarks what restrictions there are on what the franchisee can do what fees the franchisee will pay how you will help the franchisee initially - eg training what continuing support you will provide - eg National marketing campaigns or administrative support how long the franchise lasts and what happens at the end of the term what happens if either of you wants to bring the agreement to an end or sell your business.

A good agreement strikes a balance between the two of you. If the agreement is too one-sided in your favour, it will be difficult to attract potential franchisees. For more information on what franchisees look for in a franchise agreement, see our guide on how to buy a franchise.

Franchise agreements involve complex legal issues. You should take advice from a lawyer with franchising expertise.

2.2.3 Master franchises

Also known as master licenses or inbound franchises are franchise opportunities that have proven themselves in their home country but have no presence as yet in the UK. It will be your job as the master franchise owner to bring the franchise system into the UK. Before you do so, you need to evaluate potential benefits against obvious risks and understand the steps to buying a master franchise.

2.3.4 Invest in a Master Franchise

Before investing in a master franchise, like any business opportunity or investment, you need to be certain that becoming a master franchisee is right for you.

You need to be sure what type of franchise best suits your investment limitations, experience, and goals. For example, if you want to operate just one outlet, a master franchise is not for you.

You will need to establish if the local market is ready for the product or service. In other words, you need to ensure that there are enough people around who want to purchase it and, most importantly, can actually afford it.

You need to be careful and patient. Wait for the right deal with the right company. Walk away from any deal where full information is not provided or the foreign franchisor applies pressure on you to sign the agreement. Terminate negotiations with any foreign franchisor that is not prepared to enter into a joint commitment to develop the local market.

Be prepared to accept that even once you have found the right franchise partner it will still take a long time to close the deal.

Lastly, you need to ask yourself whether the potential of the deal justifies the initial expenses and ongoing costs. Remember, you will be obliged to;

- Pay a license fee, which may be substantial
- Fund the establishment and operation of the local pilot operation
- Either creates the franchise infrastructure, from scratch or you may have to modify the master franchisor's material to suit local requirements. Chances are that this will, among other things, involve significant professional fees
- Adapt the product or service to suit local conditions
- Attend initial and ongoing training at the master franchisor's head office, thus incurring initial and ongoing travel expenses that can be substantial
- Share initial and ongoing fees with the foreign master franchisor. In this context, you need to keep in mind that for practical purposes, fee

levels may be pegged, forcing you to make ends meet with only a portion of the gross income your local competitors earn

Before you go any further, you need to decide whether it is indeed worth your while to invest in the master franchise. Perhaps it would make more sense to develop a concept locally from scratch. In most instances, unless the master franchise offers you access to an internationally renowned brand or extraordinary intellectual capital, the local option may be preferable.

2.2.5 Master Franchise Mistakes

Below is a list of points that franchisors should consider when looking to franchise internationally. This should help them to avoid making mistakes later.

- Perfect your concept before you go abroad
- Get all your documentation up to date and be prepared to adapt it to the new country
- Don't over extend yourself ; Do only one country at a time
- Common language is a huge benefit
- Research the local market and the locals know better
- Even raw materials are different from country to country
- Budget accurately and allocate costs correctly; Setting up a master franchise properly is expensive
- The correct master franchisee is essential not just the personality but
- does he have sufficient capital ; Strict guidance and control is needed in the beginning
- Training is an essential part of success – even to extend the company culture
- Ensure good marketing
- Under pressure; It's difficult to keep the master franchisee motivated

2.3 Social Enterprise

A social enterprise is an organization that applies business strategies to achieving philanthropic goals. Social enterprises can be structured as a for-profit or non-profit.

Social enterprises are distinct from charities (although charities are also increasingly looking at ways of maximizing income from trading), and from private sector companies with policies on corporate social responsibility. An emerging view, however, is that social enterprise is a particular type of trading activity that sometimes gives rise to distinct organization forms reflecting a commitment to social cause working with stakeholders from more than one sector of the economy.

The national body for the social enterprise movement in Britain is the Social Enterprise Coalition (SEC) and this liaises with similar groups in each region of England, and in Northern Ireland, Scotland & Wales. The definition of social enterprise propagated by the SEC is slightly broader than the original DTI definition and acknowledged that the social purpose of an organisation can be 'embedded in its structure and governance'. As such, social businesses that adopt inclusive governance structures and employee-ownership are brought fully into the fold of the movement.

In the British context, social enterprises include community enterprises, credit unions, trading arms of charities, employee-owned businesses, co-operatives, development trusts, housing associations, social forms, and leisure trusts.

Many commercial enterprises would consider themselves to have social objectives, but commitment to these objectives is fundamentally motivated by the perception that such commitment will ultimately make the enterprise more financially valuable. Social enterprises differ in that, inversely, they do not aim to offer any benefit to their investors, except where they believe that doing so will ultimately further their capacity to realise their philanthropic goals.

Many entrepreneurs, whilst running a profit focused enterprise that they own, will make charitable gestures through the enterprise, expecting to make a loss in the process. However unless the social aim is the primary purpose of the company this is not considered to be social enterprise. The term is more specific, meaning 'doing charity *by* doing trade', rather than 'doing charity *while* doing trade'. Another example is an incorporation, which may pursue social responsibility goals that conflict with traditional corporate shareholder primacy, or may donate most of its profits to charity.

2.3.1 Examples

- Unincorporated Associations
- Trusts
- Limited Companies
- Community Benefit Societies
- Community Interest Companies
- Charitable Incorporated Organizations

2.3.2 Unincorporated associations

The unincorporated association form is usually chosen when a number of individuals agree or 'contract' to come together for a common purpose - which may be of a social nature.

Unincorporated associations may also have trading or business objectives or carry on commercial activities.

2.3.3 Trusts

They are a legal device, which governs how assets given by an individual or organisation are to be used. Many organisations, such as those involved in education, healthcare, providing advice and conservation, can be structured as trusts.

There is no standard legal form for a development trust. Most register as a company limited by guarantee and in a few cases as an industrial and provident society.

2.3.4 Limited companies with a social purpose

The limited company is an organisational structure which gives limited liability to its members. Some social enterprises take on the form of a limited company. This is a more accountable form than, for example, an unincorporated association.

Limited companies may have an 'objects' clause that sets out the company's aims or purposes. Although these objects can be commercial, if your business is a social enterprise, they must also relate to social and/or environmental objectives such as regenerating an area or providing employment and/or training for people disadvantaged in the labour market. Social enterprises that are registered charities must only have objects that the law defines as charitable, such as relieving financial hardship or promoting education.

2.3.5 Community Benefit Societies

(BenComs) are incorporated industrial and provident societies (IPS) that conduct business for the benefit of their community. Profits are not distributed among members, or external shareholders, but returned to the community. For example, a nursery school might use this form to let staff take part in decision-making.

As IPS, some key characteristics of BenComs are as follows;

- They are set up with social objectives to conduct a business or trade.
- They are run and managed by their members.
- They must submit annual accounts.

Some well known social enterprises in the UK include John Lewis, Welsh Water, Cafedirect, The Eden Project, Divine Chocolate(Kuapa Kokoo), The Big Issue, the Co-operative Group, HCT Group, Duchy Originals, and the London Symphony Orchestra.

Three common characteristics of social enterprises as defined by Social Enterprise London are;

- Enterprise orientation; they are directly involved in producing goods or providing services to a market. They seek to be viable trading organizations, with an operating surplus.
- Social Aims: They have explicit social aims such as job creation, training, or the provision of local services. They have ethical values including a commitment to local capacity building, and they are accountable to their members and the wider community for their social environmental and economic impact.
- Social ownership; They are autonomous organisations with governance and ownership structures based on participation by stakeholder groups (users or clients, local community groups etc.) or by trustees. Profits are distributed as profit sharing to stakeholders or used for the benefit of the community.

2.3.6 Community Interest Company

The UK has also developed a new legal form called the community interest company (CIC). CICs are a new type of limited company designed specifically for those wishing to operate for the benefit of the community rather than for the benefit of the owners of the company. This means that a CIC cannot be formed or used solely for the personal gain of a particular person, or group of people. Legislation caps the level of dividends payable at 35% of profits and returns to individuals are capped at 4% above the bank base rate.

CICs can be limited by shares, or by guarantee, and will have a statutory 'asset lock' to prevent the assets and profits being distributed, except as permitted by legislation. This ensures the assets and profits are retained within the CIC for community purposes, or transferred to another asset-locked organisation, such as another CIC or charity.

A CIC cannot be formed to support political activities and a company that is a charity cannot be a CIC, unless it gives up its charitable status. However, a charity may apply to register a CIC as a subsidiary company.

2.3.7 Social firms

Another example of a type of social enterprise is the social firm, a business set up specifically to create employment for people otherwise severely disadvantaged in the labour market.

2.4 Advantages of social enterprise

- Ability to raise capital at below market rates due to the ethical
- Investment industry
- Easier access to publicity
- Labour cost below average, 'as staff seems willing to work forbelow market rates in support of the values of social enterprises.'

CHAPTER THREE

THE BUSINESS PLAN

Introduction

A Business Plan explains what you hope to do, how much money you need to do it with and how you propose to pay the money back. Your plan will include a Profit Forecast and Cash Flow Model.

However, there is more to the Business Plan than getting funding. It will help you clarify your ideas and objectives. You will have to answer questions on your business objectives, your product or service, pricing methods, your customers and competition. (Many Franchisors will assist in the preparation of a business plan)

3.1 Preparing your business plan

- Describe the purpose of your Business, briefly outline the concept.
- Include YOUR overall business objectives.
- Decide on the 'legal status' of your business - sole trader, partnership, limited company or co-operative? All have benefits and shortcomings. Find out which is right for your situation.
- Summary business description - details of the franchise being purchased and the financial needs.
- Market analysis & product / service - research and identify local competition and assess what the likely demand of the product / service will be in the specific territory.

- Market Strategy - outline intentions for marketing the product / service and how the sales figures shown in the projections will be generated.
- Management plan - include details of the type of business (e.g., sole trader, limited company) and CVs of key personnel. Set out the structure and key skills of the management team and staff.
- Financial data - at least two years projected figures are required, including a balance sheet, cash flow and profit & loss statement, ensuring that projections correspond with the information outlined above and they're realistic. If it is a resale franchise, include details of the existing business being sold. Has the business been growing? Is it profitable? A copy of previous years' accounts should also be included.

SWOT analysis - a one-page analysis of strengths, weaknesses, opportunities and threats.

To summarise, here are our fundamental rules for writing a plan;

Do;

- Clarify the purpose of your plan before you write it
- Focus on the key information the reader will want
- Highlight future plans as well as describing the current situation
- Be realistic

Don't;

- Waffle or include unnecessary detail
- Base your plan on over-optimistic assumptions

Your Bank will be interested in your long-term forecasts - but your family will be equally interested in your short-term projections. Will you be able to afford a holiday next year? What will your standard of living be?

Preparing, presenting, and defending your business plan is a real test of your business acumen. Producing the plan tends to bring everything out into the open, focuses your mind on all elements of the business, and helps put your thoughts down in black and white.

Your Business Plan is the 'sales document' for you and your business. It's preparation and presentation should project the image you want for your business. Its content should be clear, concise, to the point and divided into logical sections.

3.2 The Product or Service

- Describe precisely the product or service that your business will offer. Include any relevant history of the product or service and try to avoid any jargon.
- List the distinctive qualities of your product or service and describe your 'Unique Selling Point' (USP) - the key feature which makes your product or service stand out in the market place.
- Describe how your product or service can be developed in line with a changing market.

3.3 The Personnel

'Any business is only as good as its people.' You should include details of anyone who will be involved in making your business a success. These people are a very important asset and this is therefore a key section of your Business Plan.

- A précis of each person, including their personal assessment of their attributes, strengths, and weaknesses as well as your own assessment of each person.
- Their relevant experience, commitment, and reasons for involvement in your new venture.
- You should also include a detailed CV for each person in the 'Appendix' at the end of your plan.

3.4 The Market

This is probably the most important section of the whole Plan - without a clearly defined market your business will not succeed. If you can show that you have 'done your homework' in this section, you will gain credibility for the whole Business plan. Your franchisor will also have research in this area.

- Describe the current conditions in the market place for your product or service.
- Detail any relevant facts and figures relating to the market sector(s) that you will be targeting - for example geographical location, size (in terms of people and money), expected growth, and the type(s) of potential customers for your product or service.
- Give details of your competitors and explain why your potential customers will choose your product or service rather than the competition.

This is the point where research pays off. You should make use of the wealth of business information that is available about markets, competitors and customers.

3.5 The Marketing Plan

A business without a Marketing Plan is like a ship without a rudder. Your company must therefore have a clearly defined marketing plan, which will include;

- Your marketing objectives - for example number of sales or market share.

- Where your product or service will be 'positioned' in the market place in terms of price, quality, image etc.

- What your planned marketing communications are - advertising, leaflets and brochures, etc.

- How your product or service will be distributed and /or sold eg. Through agents, sales teams, etc.

- What customer care policy is planned and how it will work.

Any interest that you have already generated or details of possible orders you have already taken should be include in the appendix.

3.6 The Operation

Having an efficient operation can be the key to a profitable business. Describe how you will supply your product and which channels are you going to use to promote or advertise your products. Include your sources .

CHAPTER FOUR

EXAMINING THE ORGANIZATION

Introduction

This is an essential step in ensuring that your organisation really understands who its key customers are, what they need, and that appropriate resources are then used to make sure that the potential from these key customers is realised.

4.1 The organisation's potential customer base

Identifying and prioritising potential customer groups, and therefore informing how your products should be marketed and sold. It includes evaluating the potential of key customer groups, and identifying priority groups based upon a realistic review of their forecast financial return.

4.2 The needs and expectations of the organisation

As businesses grow, they go through different phases of development. The entrepreneur needs to handle each stage differently.

For example, in a new business, you might focus on producing your products (or services) and selling to new customers. In a small business like this, you might not feel the need to spend much time managing the business - everyone knows what they are supposed to do and gets on with it.

However, an approach like this will only take you so far. As the business grows, you need to start acting more as a leader, and shifting your attention towards activities such as managing employee performance and developing the right strategy for the future. As well as changing your approach, this may well involve learning new management skills.

Recognising what stage of development your business has reached is an important part of ensuring that it achieves its growth potential. You need to understand what skills and behaviors will help take the business forward and make sure that those are the ones you provide. Be ready to change when necessary to help the business move to the next phase.

Understanding your own preferences and how you tend to run your business can help with this. See the page in this guide on your entrepreneurial personality.

4.3 Actual and potential competitors

To market your business confidently you will need to learn how your product or service fits into the current market, how your business is operating in the current economic climate, and any positives and negatives of your competitors.

Understanding your existing and potential customers, the product or service's marketplace and who your competition is, allows you to plan for;

- Targeting your customers
- Selling effectively
- Competing with other suppliers
- Discovering new business opportunities

Conducting market research on your potential customers, or researching your competitors, can help you to plan your next marketing move and take advantage of any competitor weaknesses. It will also help you to understand potential and existing customers.

Market research and marketing reports can show;

- The demand for your product or service
- The current overall economic and market trends
- Customer requirements and buying behaviours
- Any new upcoming products from a competitor
- Competitor changes in operations
- Competitor products and prices
- Competitor PR and advertising strategies
- Any upcoming legislation that could affect your market

To learn about how knowledge of your competition can help your business, see our guide on competing in markets dominated by big brands.

4.4 Actual and potential partners

When choosing a joint venture partner, you should consider;

- Existing customers and suppliers, competitors and professional associates as partners
- Whether the culture of a proposed partner fits with that of your organisation
- Whether the finances of the proposed partner organisation are sound potential for overseas sales or activities

4.4.1 Finance

You should prepare the following documents for a joint venture;

- Business plan
- Marketing plan
- Cashflow projection

Each partner should agree who is investing what, and in what form - eg cash or other assets.

If external funding is needed, the partners should agree;

- Sources of funding, eg a share issue
- Who will borrow the funds
- How the borrowing will be guaranteed

Arrangements for profit and loss should be agreed, eg;

- How any profits or losses should be divided
- How capital gains or losses should be divided; whether one partner will be paid for providing services, other than through a share of profits

4.4.2 Implementing a joint venture

When you are ready to implement a joint venture, you should make a joint venture agreement including;

- Clear business objectives
- Communication arrangements between organisations/teams
- Financial arrangements
- Protection of your interests, eg trade secrets
- Day-to-day and strategic decision making

- Whether either party can pursue other business during the joint venture
- Dispute resolution procedures

Decide on a legal structure for your joint venture, eg;

- Contractual co-operation for a defined project
- Partnership or unlimited partnership
- Limited liability company
- Full merger of the two organisations

Bank account arrangements will depend on the legal model chosen, although a new account can be set up for a single project. You should agree;

- In whose name account(s) are set up
- Arrangements for depositing or withdrawing funds, including co-signatories

4.4.3 Sourcing business together

You should agree in advance which organisation has responsibility for;

- Sales activities
- Marketing activities
- New business generation

Such arrangements should be specified in the joint venture business and marketing plans.

4.4.4 Terminating the joint venture

The agreement needs to make provision for terminating the agreement, covering;

- Termination procedure
- Ownership of assets in the joint venture
- Allocation of any liabilities resulting from the joint venture

4.5 The organisation's performance

There is no doubt that a good organization with a poor equipment will give better results than the best equipment with a poor organization. Energy and enthusiasm help to be more focused to achieve goals in a more efficient manner. You would find less troubles being organized. Some people are too lazy unable to be tidy with the paper work.

Do not waste your space, working in a messy place you will find it is hard to concentrate. If you can manage your stuff in order, things are a lot easier and lessen anxiety. Being organized you will handle incoming mail and papers quickly when you need them.

Keep one agenda with calendar for all your appointments, timelines, deadlines, and activities. Enter the things to do for the coming day, week schedule. Make a list of the things you need along with a budget amount for each item so you don't overspend. Do not spend more than you can afford.

4.5.1 Pros/Cons

Many problems have several solutions, each of which must be weighed before a decision is made. Conducting a logical analysis of the pros and cons of an issue is thus important in organizing.

4.5.2 Communication skills

Time is too valuable to permit of prolonged speaking. Men are tacitly expect ed to 'get to the point,' and to be reasonably brief in what they have to say.

Receivers or listeners show interest only if the person communicating is loaded   with confidence, gestures, and softness.

Communication skills include courtesy, social confidence, tact, mutual understanding, cooperation, and trust.

These skills are the key to executing good management. Internal obstacles fo r a good coomunication are fear, shame and anger.

If English is not your first language, speaking in foreign language is actually even more difficult than writing; while writing you can pause and go to the dictionaries or rearrange the sentence but that is quite impossible in normal conversation where, instead, you're just stumped and get these awkward pauses not knowing what to say or how to phrase it.

We all know that English is the global language, but orders must be given to the employees in detail in writing; and in order to lay out the next day's work and plan the entire progress of work through the shop. Daily reports must be made by the team leaders, or supervisors in writing, showing just what has been done.

4.6 Packaging

Most food products are stored, distributed and marketed in packaging of some kind. Food also comes into contact with many different surfaces - both in the home and in commercial settings. It is therefore very important that the materials used in packaging are regulated and monitored to ensure they're safe in different situations and with different types of food product.

4.7 Managing Waste

The purpose of managing waste is to promote the economic use of materials / resources and methods so that waste is minimised. Any waste produced in an organisation should be reused, recycled or recovered in some other ways before disposing of any waste.

Currently, it is claimed that there is a cost of £15 billion to British industry because of bad waste practices. By minimizing waste in the workplace, significant financial savings can be made, as well as reducing the impact of the business on the environment. The key areas of potential physical waste are;

- Misuse
- Extravagance
- Rework
- Shrinkage

Waste can be reduced in the workplace by implementing the following practices;

Paper consumption - Can be reduced by using double-sided photocopying, 'waste' sheets as scrap paper and email wherever possible, only printing off emails when necessary. Post visual reminders around the organisation reminding employees to consider alternatives to producing waste

Publications - Try not to over-order.

Amnesty Days - The aim of which is to give up items that can be reused elsewhere and to identify wastes that can be recycled. It also raises employee awareness about how much waste is unnecessarily produced.

Negotiate waste packaging with suppliers - Encourage suppliers to recover and reuse packaging a number of times before disposal. Make the best use of the available recycling facilities to minimise waste. Make sure contracts are in place to recycle glass, fluorescent tubes, paper, aluminium cans, plastics, toner cartridges, batteries, I.T. and electronic equipment and mobile phones.

Recycle - This is reprocessing used materials that would otherwise become waste. Recycling breaks down waste to reproduce new products, whereas reuse is about collecting waste to be cleaned, refilled and resold.

Recycling prevents waste from being sent to landfill sites or burned by incinerators; it reduces the consumption of new raw materials and requires less energy than producing new products. Common materials that can be recycled include;

- Glass
- Paper
- Aluminium
- Asphalt
- Steel
- Textiles
- Plastic

There are some materials that cannot be recycled or, as waste, need to follow special procedures for disposing of them. These are called hazardous materials. Hazardous materials should be disposed of safely following these procedures;

- Identify the hazardous substances in the workplace and the potential risks they pose to people's health or the environment
- Decide what precautions are needed to eliminate the risks

- Eliminate the hazardous substances wherever possible or control exposure to protect the health of the environment
- Implement control measures or procedures which employees use consistently to avoid any risks to health
- Monitor exposure
- Implement health surveillance, e.g. medical checks for employees
- Prepare plans and procedures to deal with accidents, incidents and emergencies
- Train and supervise employees to make sure that their health is not damaged when using or when coming into contact with hazardous substances

Examples of hazardous wastes include;

- Asbestos
- Lead-acid batteries
- Used engine oils and oil filters
- Solvents and solvent-based substances
- Chemical waste
- Pesticides
- Fluorescent light tubes
- Computers
- Medicines

Legislation that covers the management of waste and hazardous materials are;

- The Environmental Protection Act
- Hazardous Waste (England and Wales) Regulations 2005

Managers are duty bound to make sure hazardous waste is correctly identified at each stage of production. They must implement procedures to protect the health of employees and contractors who transport or dispose of waste. This is covered by the Health and Safety at Work Act 1974 and the Control of Substances Hazardous to Health Regulations (COSHH) 1999 (SI 1999 No. 437).

CHAPTER FIVE

RECRUITMENT

Introduction

The employer may have a dedicated human resource function to conduct the recruitment process, or he may transfer these responsibilities to line managers and supervisors. During the recruitment process all should be aware of the principles of Ethical Code, *(see chapter six)* also recruiters need to be informed of changes in the labour market to ensure that their recruitment applications are not wasted.

5.1   Top 5 Questions During an Interview

One question to always ask is; 'why do you want to work for us/why should I select you over other candidates?'

Do not necessarily look for a specific answer, but more about the quality of their thinking and their self-directness.

Always look for personal responsibility and personal competency. Those questions can tell you a lot about both...

An additional question might be directed at managing difficult situations, change, and developing resiliency. Ideally, organizations would like to have employees who develop skills to manage difficult situations without upsetting business performance too much; 'what is the greatest obstacle/change you've had to overcome in your previous/current work?' or 'what is the most difficult thing you've had to learn to improve your personal effectiveness?'

It's very hard to get to the authentic candidate - hopefully with all of these questions we can get to open, honest responses that help us determine if the candidate can and will do the job.

There are many conversation starters, but the questions that give me the best information are;

- Could you pls give a brief description of yourself?
- What is it about this position that moved you to apply?
- In your career so far, what is your 'shining moment'?
- Describe your ideal manager
- What is the most important lesson you have learned that would give you an edge in this work?
- Why did you leave your last employer?
- What mistake did you learn the most from -- what happened and what did you learn?
- Who was your greatest boss (company) and why and the inverse who was your least favourite boss or company and why?
- Tell me about a time that you loved your work and the inverse tell me about a time that you hated coming in to work?
- What is your greatest achievement in your previous position?

When interviewing face to face, you want to get to know someone as the candidate. I want to look beyond the way they are dressed and the facade they are taught to project. This can only happen as someone is relaxed. From their answer, you can continue to probe their abilities, passion, communication, and success.

Showing interest in an individual and getting them to open up is far more important than anything else in the interview.

5.2 The Equality and Human Rights Commission

The accomplishment of a company is determined by the correct number of personnel, with the suitable aptitude and abilities. For general work in a shop, there is a not required especial brain, only routine work and physical strength is necessary for a regular day of work. Identifying and planning to get the best person for the job, you have to remind that you must treat all candidates fairly and avoid discrimination.

The Equality Act 2010 sets out the legal requirements for employers. Also remind that The Equality and Human Rights Commission warns against such practices where the personnel is mainly one racial group or sex.

5.2.1 Diversity

Employment no longer caters for a clearly defined single group of people. It is a mix of people from different races, nationalities and religions. When people from diverse backgrounds enter an organisation, they bring with them their experience of different cultures and values.

Diversity refers to the different human qualities exhibited from different groups of people. Diversity in the workforce means employing people without discrimination based on gender, age and ethnic or racial background. Diversity also relates to issues of;

- Disability
- Religion
- Job title
- Physical appearance

- Sexual orientation

5.4.3 Advertising your vacancies

Before considering any costs of the advertising your vacancies you need to know exactly where your ads will be seen as well as how many times they will be shown.

Advertising your vacancies in the national press sometimes is expensive. The newspaper office will often advise on suitable formats. Advertisements should always be clear and easy to understand. They must be non discriminatory, and should avoid any gender or culturally specific language. To support this, the organisation should include in the advert its statement of commitment to equal opportunities and ethical code.

Advertisements need to make clear how applicants are going to respond, by telephone, by email, by letter, application form, fax, in person at the organisation or agency, by tape or Braille.

5.4 Small Business Recruitment Service

Working in partnership with Jobcenterplus have its advantages: Free job advertising on one of the UK's biggest job sites for free. You can get help writing your job ads and find you the right candidates making sure your job ads attract the best candidates and help you identify the right person for the job, recruiting people from your local community.

Employer Direct is a free service from Jobcentre Plus – the largest database of job vacancies in Britain- that allows you to advertise vacancies onto electronic touch-screen terminals in Jobcentre Plus offices and in local communities across Britain. Also allows employers to notify their vacancies online.

To use the Employer Direct service, contact Jobcentre Plus with details of your vacancy by;

Telephone - 0845 601 2001

Textphone for people with speech or hearing impairments - 0845 601 2002

E-mail - employerdirect-vacancies@jobcentreplus.gsi.gov.uk

5.5 Large Business Recruitment Service; Work Trials

A Work Trial is a Jobcentre Plus service that lets you try out a potential employee at no cost to your business, before you decide whether to make them a job offer.

A Work Trial gives you time to find out how well suited a person is to the job, your company culture and workforce, as well as giving the potential employee the time to decide if a job is right for them.

Nearly half of all jobs beginning with a Work Trial have led to the candidate being offered a job for the longer term.

A Work Trial is suitable for;

- Most permanent jobs over 16 hours a week that are expected to last at least three months
- Temporary jobs lasting at least three months

The person must meet certain eligibility criteria that will be checked by Jobcentre Plus. They will continue to receive their benefit, plus some expenses which Jobcentre Plus will pay.

What can Work Trials do for your business?; Work Trials are particularly successful in industries that typically have high staff turnover rates. High staff turnover can be due to a range of factors, including working conditions and hours.

The main business benefits of Work Trials are;

- They give you the time to be sure that you have the right person for the job
- They are free, there are no wage costs associated with them and Jobcentre Plus pays the person's benefit during the trial
- You won't have to fill in any tax and National Insurance paperwork until you're sure you have the right person for the job

How to arrange a Work Trial;

You can arrange to offer your vacancy as a Work Trial when you first contact Jobcentre Plus with the vacancy details. If you have already contacted Jobcentre Plus about a vacancy that you would now like to offer as a Work Trial, speak to your local contact to discuss your options.

A person looking for work may also ask their adviser whether your vacancy might be available as a Work Trial. If the adviser agrees, they will attach a brief Work Trials cover note to their application or CV.

If you decide to offer a vacancy as a Work Trial, you will need to sign a standard agreement with Jobcentre Plus. Once this is signed, you will be able to offer as many vacancies as Work Trials as you wish. Also free employee work trials For further information contact 0845 601 2001.

5.6   Pre-employment ID Check Process

Registered Bodies play an important role in the provision of the CRB checking service, in particular they must;

- Check and validate the information provided by the applicant on the application form / continuation sheet; and
- Establish the true identity of the applicant, through the examination of a range of documents as set out in this guidance; and
- Ensure that the applicant provides details of all names by which they have been known and all addresses where they have lived in the last 5 years; and
- Ensure the application form is fully completed and the information it contains is accurate.

If there are any discrepancies in the information that the applicant has provided and/or the identity documents supplied and fraud is not suspected please seek clarification from the applicant. Failure to do this may compromise the integrity of the CRB service.

Do not attempt to amend the application form without the applicant's knowledge and agreement as it will invalidate the declaration by the applicant in Section e of the form and may breach data protection legislation.

If you suspect that you have been presented with a false identity or documents at the time of application, do not proceed with the application process.

To report suspected identity fraud you can phone 0300 123 2040 or visit www.actionfraud.org.uk and for further information on identity fraud visit www.met.police.uk/fraudalert

If you suspect identity fraud once a CRB check has been submitted, you must contact the CRB by phone; 0870 90 90 811 or visit http://www.crb.homeoffice.gov.uk

5.7 Employing Immigrant Workers

You are also advised that under Section 8 of the Asylum and Immigration Act 1996 all employers in the United Kingdom are required to make basic document checks to help prevent anyone from working illegally. By carrying out checks employers will be able to establish a defence for themselves if any of their employees are found to be working illegally at a later date.

If you have concerns about the validity of documents presented to you, you should contact the Home Office Employers' Helpline on 0845 010 6677. They will treat any information you provide in confidence and pass this on to the relevant Immigration Service Local Enforcement Office for further investigation.

Often there may be criminal offences other than production of a forged document involved. If you suspect that this is the case, you should contact your local Police, who in turn will contact the local Enforcement Office. Further details are available at www.employingmigrantworkers.org.uk and the UK Border Agency Employer Helpline on 0845 010 6677

5.8 Payroll services

BACS (Bankers' Automated Clearing Services) payment is a quick, easy and effective way to make direct payments to employees, HMRC and trade suppliers, without the need for expensive hardware or software. BACS is one of the most popular payment solutions. BACS payments take three working days to clear: they are entered into the system on the first day, processed on the second day, and cleared on the third day.

Below there is a guide of a few payrollservices' providers.

WisBACS is simple and easy to use, can create BACS files and offers fully automatic recovery of problem transmissions, will link to all popular Payroll

& Accounts systems, validates sort codes and account numbers. Visit http://www.wisbacs.co.uk

Moorepay aim to give you the flexibility to design the service that you want, which is why we offer numerous types of payroll software for small businesses with up to 25 employees. These include online small business payroll software, basic managed payroll, and BACS services. Visit http://www.moorepay.co.uk

Ceridian is the UK's leading provider of Human Resource Management and Payroll Services. Visit http://www.ceridian.co.uk

5.9 Understanding Employees

Conversations about working in a shop sometimes are not very positive. It's completely normal to gripe about work occasionally. After all, there is no other social situation where people are obliged to spend a set amount of hours in the company of people they may not always like, doing things they may not always agree with.

Most of the employees spend a significant proportion of their waking hours at work, so no one wants to be stuck in an uninspiring or stressful role. While even the most satisfied employee can have an off day, it may be heartening to know that 48% of Brits describe themselves as fulfilled at work and almost two thirds.

5.9.1 The Take Easy Workmen

The slow pace which some workmen adopt, may be called the take easy. This slow pace proceeds from two causes: first from their natural instinct and tendency to take easy, which may be called making time and second from their relations with other men, which may make the slow pace systematic , only with external pressure they can take a more rapid pace. The natural laziness of men can be serious if it is done without the knowledge of the employer.

This common tendency to 'take it easy' is greatly increased by bringing a number of men together on similar work and at the same standard rate of pay by the day. Under this plan the better men gradually and surely will slow down their speed to that of the poorest and barely efficient.

5.9.2 The Hardly Workmen

There are of course men of unusual energy, vitality, ambition, motivation, set up their own standards, and who work very hard, even though it may be for abode their own interests. These men only serve to emphasize the tendency of the average.

When a naturally energetic man works for a few days beside a lazy one, the logic of the situation is unanswerable; 'Why should I work hard when that lazy fellow gets the same pay that I do and does only half as much work?'

The hardly and competent workman can be found in any large establishment, when a employer is convinced that the workman is capable of doing more work than he has done, he will find sooner or later some way of compelling him to do it with little or no increase of pay, but whether working by the day or on casual work, contract work or under any of the ordinary systems of compensating labor, who does not devote a considerable part of his time to studying just also how slowly he could work? and still convince his employer that he is going at a reasonable good pace.

5.9.3 Employees respond better to incentives

There are many factors to consider when assessing happiness at work - some of which are hard to measure -- but there's no doubting that money is a key issue and it's normal for the employees to expect salary to increase over time. Money and promotions aside, most people prefer to be stimulated at work and boredom is often cited as a key reason for leaving a job. Doing the same role, day after day for several years, can become extremely tedious and leave you feeling jaded and in need of a new focus.

Employers derive their knowledge of how much of a given type of work can be done in a period of time from either their own experience, or from casual and systematic observation of their men, or at best from records which are kept, showing, the quickest time in which each job has been done.

In many cases the employer will feel almost certain that a given job can be done faster than it has been in the past for them to make new records under the stimulus of the incentive, moving toward a higher rate of speed which result in temporarily increasing the workers' wages, then the systematically take easy gait can be broke, but later on all those new who come after them are made to work harder for the same old pay.

The recent economic climate has forced numerous organisations to freeze pay rises and promotions until their financial situation improves. However, Home Learning College research shows that 10% of workers have not had a pay rise in the past five years -- long before the recession caused companies to tighten the purse strings.

CHAPTER SIX

Ethical Code of Conduct

Introduction

- Understand how to treat other people at work
- Understand how to maintain security and confidentiality at work
- Be able to respect and support other people at work in an organisation
- Be able to maintain security and confidentiality
- Be able to keep waste to a minimum and follow procedures for disposal and recycling

6.1 Respect- Employers, managers or leaders shall treat employees with equality, dignity and politeness, and always conscious of how their decisions may affect them.

The company shall have a commitment of respect towards all of its employees and ensure that employees show this respect in their relations with other employees. The company has a commitment of respect towards different communities and environments.

6.2 Politeness- As a rule employers never should underestimated the employees and members of the public. No one in the workplace never have to be unjustly treated verbally or physically.

Members who as employers or managers shall have a commitment of respect to all their employees all the time and so the employees.

The employers and managers have two show - respect and politeness - towards all of its employees and the different environment and communities in which operates.

6.3   Honesty- Everyone involved with the organization and   in the workplace shall act with honesty and integrity rejecting cynics and criticism. Honesty is the key to building quality relationships, which is important in any working environment.

Employers and employees shall conduct all the services honestly and honourably, expecting the customers and suppliers to do the same.

With advice, strategic assistance and the methods imparted through training everyone involve in the company shall take proper account of ethical considerations, together with the protection and enhancement of the moral position of the customers and suppliers.

6.4   Integrity- All members of the company shall try always to behave in the correct way following the values of the Code. Always obeying the law, the Code and the internal and external rules, policies and processes established.

Employers shall make sure that employees understand what they have to do and how to do it meeting training needs if necessary.

Also considering working flexible hours would help employees to manage demands.

6.5   Performance- Members as a employers, managers, team leaders and employees involved in the organization must take steps to ensure that their private, personal, political and financial interests do not conflict with their professional duties. They shall perform their duties fearlessly and impartially and exercise their independent professional judgment to the best.

Employers shall notify the their employees instructions in writing before undertaking work   and shall satisfy themselves that the necessary instructions have been received and the employees should ensure that the services offered are appropriate to their professional requirements.

The organization may from time to time publish supplementary regulations relating to such matters as continuing professional development, planning aid, professional indemnity insurance, professional promotions, or direct professional access to the premises etc... In addition, employees shall comply with any such regulations.

6.6 Equality Rights- Shall not discriminate on the grounds of race, sex, creed, age, religion, or disability and shall seek to eliminate such discrimination by others and promote equality opportunity.

The Equality Act 2010 sets out the legal requirements for employers. Also remind that The Equality and Human Rights Commission warns. against such practices where the personnel is mainly one racial group or sex.

6.7 Natural Environment- The company is responsible towards the natural environment and shall make efforts to preserve it in all the activities.

6.8 Community- To wish respect to local customs and bring value to the communities where the company do business.

6.9 Labor Conditions- To observe responsible recruitment practices not employing under abusive conditions.

Reject any form of child labor.

Employees are promoted based on their merits and competences providing a safe environment, which complies with health and safety measures at workplace.

Employees must observe safety regulations and not endanger colleagues or premises.

6.10 Flexibility- All the members in the company should be capable of adapting to challenges and opportunities open to new ways of seeing things.

6.11 Work Appreciation and Encouragement - Employers or managers that have responsibility for other members in the company shall take all reasonable steps to encourage and support such other members in the maintenance of professional performance.

6.12 Anger Management - All the members involved in the company shall eexpress the emotions without hurting others and learning to control anger and express it appropriately, it will help to build better relationships between employers and employees and members of the public, achieving goals, leading healthier and having more satisfying life.

6.11 Excellence - Employers and Employees shall know their stuff and be highly skilled by keeping up with the latest knowledge and techniques believing that everything can be done still better with better results. Learning from the past to avoid repeating the same mistakes demanding always the highest possibly quality of work.

6.12 Engagement - Before commencing work employees shall ensure that their terms of engagement have been given and confirmed in writing and shall satisfy themselves that all the terms included the Ethical Code Standard have been accepted.

Employers may have the willing to engage the employees combining inspirational coach and a motivational leadership to force employees to become and remain ambitious and energetic, rewarding and noticing their efforts giving them sufficient pay to live better than in the past to become prosperous.

6.13 Redundancy- If you do not need an employee working with you be polite and honest and explain the reason of his/her dismissal.

6.14 Privacy Rights / Confidentiality- Members shall not disclose or authorise to be disclosed use to the advantage of themselves, their employers, or customers, confidential information acquired in confidence in the course of their work, except with the permission of a relevant authority, or at the direction of a court of law.

You should be committed to maintaining the highest degree of integrity in all our dealings with potential, current, and past clients, or both in terms of normal commercial confidentiality, and the protection of all personal information received in the course of providing the business services concerned.

You should extend the same standards to all our customers, suppliers, and associates.

6.15 Health and Safety- The Employers shall under common law to take reasonable care to ensure the health and safety of their employees. If one of the employees suffers from stress related ill-health and the court decides that the employer should have been able to prevent it, then the employer could be found to be negligent. There is no limit to the compensation the employees could get from this.

Some forms of stress can be prevented - for example, the somewhat organisational stress caused by poor management or the lack of policies for dealing with bullying. Individual stress - relating to relationships or personal problems outside work - can also be reduced with the right kind of understanding and support from employers.

All employees have a duty to assist in the creation of a safe working environment, where unacceptable behavior is not tolerated. This may include challenging

6.16 Practice of Ethical Code of Conduct - Everyone in the company shall be responsible for their own conduct. This code is the tool, which should help to resolve questions they may have regarding how they act in their daily work.

No behaviour can be justified on the basis 'everyone does it' or 'this is life'. Employers, employees, and everyone involved in the company have to be responsible for knowing and applying the Code.

Before taking a decision, everyone should consider the following questions;

- Am I being ethical?
- Am I certain that my decision does not contravene the Code?
- Might my decision prejudice other persons in the organisation?

- Is my interpretation of the Code subjective?
- Could my actions be reported as being in breach of the Code?

When doubts remain, it is important to ask for guidance, either from any direct superior, the manager responsible for Human Resources, the Legal Service or the senior business unit manager and in last extreme the council. Everyone in the company has the right to approach the person they consider most appropriate.

Employers are required to ensure that everyone involved in the company follow the Code and they know, respect and promote its contents. Employers and Employees should make efforts to ensure that the Code's values and principles are promoted amongst all interested parties, providers, suppliers, clients other companies etc...

All the business units must take the necessary measures to adopt the Code and put it into practice. All the internal regulations and policies must be coherent with the content of the Code.

Everyone involved in the company must report possible infractions of the Code, whether affecting them personally or others, following the procedure established in the section "How to report an infraction".

No employee may ask another to breach the Code, nor may an incorrect illicit action be justified by an order in contravention of the Code received from a superior.

The application of the Code presupposes the observance of all applicable legislation in every country where the company does business.

The Company reserves the right to take any legal action if considers necessary in the case of infractions of the document and/or the spirit of the Code

6.17 How to report any infraction - To report possible infractions of the Code contact the Council, once they receive your message and will be responsible for organising the investigations of any related facts, information or documents. The communication process cannot be anonymous.

The council shall offer sufficient guarantees to preserve the privacy of those who report an infraction and it would be difficult to investigate an issue thoroughly, which had been reported anonymously. The company guarantees that not employee will be prejudiced for having reported possible infraction.

Everybody in the company may cooperate with the investigative processes relating possible infractions and the company will always support any action taken in defense of the Code.

No one in the company is permitted to prevent another from reporting a possible infraction.

6.18 Disciplinary Action- If local councils are committed to helping local authorities to have resource, power and capacity to make life better in the living place they should committee as well to have power and capacity to help local authorities to make life better in the workplace.

Councils shall promote Ethical Code Standards at Workplace and to take disciplinary action only when a employer or employee or a person involved with the organization is personally responsible for the misconduct or any alleged breach of this code.

6.19 Stop Bulling- Be Calm by speaking in a low but self-confident tone. Show that you understand the immediate problem.

With your voice, tone, and body language, show them that you don't take them attack personally. For more information, please visit the web; http://nationalbullyinghelpline.co.uk

CUSTOMER SERVICES

Introduction

Customers in today's world vary enormously in terms of their social and economic conditions. Their choice of product is frequently dependent upon a complex mix of related circumstances. These include not only their life stage and affluence; but also include product offering, price sensitivities, and needs.

7.1 Consumer Protection from Unfair Trading Regulations 2008

Treating customers fairly is vital to ensuring that you win and retain customers. The Enterprise Act and the Consumer Protection from Unfair Trading Regulations are used to ensure businesses comply with it.

The Consumer Protection from Unfair Trading Regulations 2008 came into force on 26 May 2008. They implement the Unfair Commercial Practices Directive (UCPD) in the UK, and replace several pieces of consumer protection legislation that were in force prior to 26 May 2008.

The Regulations introduce a general duty not to trade unfairly and seek to ensure that traders act honestly and fairly towards their customers. They apply primarily to business to consumer practices (but elements of business to business practices are also covered where they affect, or are likely to affect, consumers).

The vast majority of UK businesses are fair dealing and should not have needed to change their business practices to comply with the Regulations, which aim to tackle those businesses who don't always treat their customers well.

For more information see the OFT/Department for Business Enterprise and Regulatory Reform (BERR) at www.oft.gov.uk

7.2 Customer Relationships

Although customer service is an important component of successful retail, it's just one of the many things that must be executed perfectly in order to continue growing. Even when customer assistants are sincere, the customers can complain that they still are not offered the kind of products or services that are appropriate for them.

The ability to maintain client relationships is one of the most important professional skills. Some techniques are explored in neuro-linguistic programming. Below there are a few examples.

7.2.1 Rapport - It is one of the most important features or characteristics of subconscious communication. It is commonality of perspective: being 'in sync' with, or being 'on the same wavelength' as the person with whom you are talking.

There are a number of techniques supposed to be beneficial in building rapport such as; matching your body language (i.e., posture, gesture, etc.); maintaining eye contact; and matching breathing rhythm.

7.2.2 Mirroring- That means getting reasonably into rhythm with the person on as many levels as possible.

7.2.3 Emotional Mirroring -Empathizing with someone's emotional state by being on 'their side'.

You must apply the skill of being a good listener in this situation so as you can listen for key words and problems that arise when speaking with the person. This is so you can talk about these issues and question them to better your understanding of what they are saying and show your empathy towards them.

7.2.4 Posture mirroring - Matching the tone of a person's body language not through direct imitation, as this can appear as mockery, but through mirroring the general message of their posture and energy.

7.2.5 Tone and Tempo Mirroring - Matching the tone, tempo, inflection, and volume of a person's voice.

7.3 Commonality - It is the technique of deliberately finding something in common with a person or a customer in order to build a sense of comradely and trust. This is done through shared interests, dislikes, and situations.

7.4 Assertive behavior

It is a 'Behavior which enables a person to act in his own best interests, to stand up for himself without undue anxiety, to express his honest feeling comfortably, or to exercise his own rights without denying the rights of others. A situation extremely difficult to predict or a personal mistake may suffer initial client backlash, but most people will appreciate the honest

7.5 Customers' returns and the law

The law gives customers some legal rights when they return items they have bought from the sellers. The main law is the Sale of Goods Act, along with some additional regulations. The Sale of Goods Act 1979 as amended;

When someone buys goods, the seller forms a contract between the buyer and the seller, which is legally binding and is covered by a law called the Sale of Goods Act 1979. Customers have the rights of returning an item to the retailer when the item they have bought is faulty;

- Does not match its description
- Is not of satisfactory quality
- Is not fit for purpose.

If any of these apply, under law the item does not conform to contract. The contract is the legal agreement the retailers have with the customer when they sell them something.

If the item is faulty for any of the reasons above, the customer has rights and they are entitled to ask to do something about the problem.

The same rights apply even if the goods are reduced in a sale or they are being sold as second-hand goods, for example, a jacket sold as a ski jacket should be warm and flexible.

For more information, please visit www.consumerdirect.gov.uk

7.6 When don't customers have rights?

The customer does not have rights under the Sale of Goods Act if;

- They accidentally damaged the item
- They misused it and caused a fault
- They tried to repair it and damaged it
- They knew it was faulty before they bought it – because the fault was clearly pointed out to them
- They've changed their mind (for example, wrong colour, doesn't suit them, found something else they like more)
- If it would not be reasonable to expect the item to have lasted this long

- If it is over six years since they bought the item, or more than five years since they discovered the problem
- If the item was bought in Scotland.

Some retailers do give refunds or exchange goods, for example, if someone has bought the wrong size, but retailers do not have to do this by law.

For further information visit www.consumerdirect.gov.uk

7.7 Retailers Responsibilities

Anything the trader say about an item, for example, advertising, labeling or advice that they give – whether it comes from manufacturers, importers, producers etc... – must be correct. These statements are part of the seller contract with the customer, for example, if the seller sells a pair of shoes that say a waterproof and the customer wears them and finds they are not, then the item is faulty (not as described).

Sellers cannot remove a customer's legal rights, for example by telling customers the sellers do not accept returns. Because the seller is the responsible to sell the goods to the customer, they are responsible for their complaint and they cannot pass this on to the manufacturer or someone else.

7.8 Refund, Repair, or Replacement?

Even when goods are faulty, a customer may not be entitled to a full refund in some instances they may not be entitled to anything at all;

- If a reasonable opportunity to inspect or reject the goods has passed
- If the seller prove the item wasn't faulty when the customer bought it (for returns under six months since purchase)

- If the customer can prove the item was faulty when they bought it (for returns over six months since purchase).

For more information, please visit Office of Fair Trade at www.oft.gov.uk

7.9 Retaining and getting more from your customers

Your customers will fall into two categories: frequent or infrequent. To get the most profit out of your current customers, you need to encourage infrequent customers to buy from you more often. This is a quicker, easier, and cheaper way to increase sales than attracting new customers.

'Customer retention strategy' is a term for the methods you use to keep existing customers and encourage them to buy from you frequently. Customer care and methods of customer retention.

7.10 Customer relationship management

There are several reasons why implementing a customer relationship management (CRM) solution might not have the desired results.

There could be a lack of commitment from people within the company to the implementation of a CRM solution. Adapting to a customer-focused approach may require a cultural change.

There is a danger that relationships with customers will break down somewhere along the line, unless everyone in the business is committed to viewing their operations from the customers' perspective. The result is customer dissatisfaction and eventual loss of revenue.

Poor communication can prevent buy-in. In order to make CRM work, all the relevant people in your business must know what information you need and how to use it.

Weak leadership could cause problems for any CRM implementation plan. The onus is on management to lead by example and push for a customer focus on every project. If a proposed plan isn't right for your customers, don't do it. Send your teams back to the drawing board to come up with a solution that will work.

Trying to implement CRM as a complete solution in one go is a tempting but risky strategy. It is better to break your CRM project down into manageable pieces by setting up pilot programs and short-term milestones.

Consider starting with a pilot project that incorporates all the necessary departments and groups but is small and flexible enough to allow adjustments along the way.

Don't underestimate how much data you will require, and make sure that you can expand your systems if necessary. You need to carefully consider what data is collected and stored to ensure that only useful data is kept.

7.10.1 How to implement CRM

The implementation of a customer relationship management (CRM) strategy is best treated as a six-stage process, moving from collecting information about your customers and processing it to using that information to improve your marketing and the customer experience.

Stage 1 - Collecting information -The priority should be to capture the information you need to identify your customers and categorize their behavior.

Those businesses with a website and online customer service have an advantage as customers can enter and maintain their own details when they buy.

Stage 2 - Storing information -The most effective way to store and manage your customer information is in a relational database - a centralized customer database that will allow you to run all your systems from the same source, ensuring that everyone uses up-to-date information.

Stage 3 - Accessing information - With information collected and stored centrally, the next stage is to make this information available to staff in the most useful format.

Stage 4 - Analysing customer behavior -Using data mining tools in spreadsheet programs, which analyse data to identify patterns or relationships, you can begin to profile customers and develop sales strategies.

Stage 5 - Marketing more effectively -Many businesses find that a small percentage of their customers generate a high percentage of their profits. Using CRM to gain a better understanding of your customers' needs, desires and self-perception, you can reward and target your most valuable customers.

Stage 6 - Enhancing the customer experience - Just as a small group of customers are the most profitable, a small number of complaining customers often take up a disproportionate amount of staff time. If their problems can be identified and resolved quickly, your staff will have more time for other customers.

7.10.2 Types of CRM solution

Customer relationship management (CRM) is important in running a successful business. The better the relationship, the easier it is to conduct business and generate revenue. Therefore using technology to improve CRM makes good business sense.

Outsourced solutions Application service providers can provide web-based CRM solutions for your business. This approach is ideal if you need to implement a solution quickly and your company does not have the in-house skills necessary to tackle the job from scratch. It is also a good solution if you are already geared towards online e-commerce. For more information see our guide on cloud computing.

Off-the-shelf solutions Several software companies offer CRM applications that integrate with existing packages. Cut-down versions of such software may be suitable for smaller businesses. This approach is generally the cheapest option as you are investing in standard software components. The downside is that the software may not always do precisely what you want and you may have to trade off functionality for convenience and price. The key to success is to be flexible without compromising too much.

Bespoke software For the ultimate in tailored CRM solutions, consultants and software engineers will customise or create a CRM system and integrate it with your existing software. However, this can be expensive and time consuming. If you choose this option, make sure you carefully specify exactly what you want. This will usually be the most expensive option and costs will vary depending on what your software designer quotes.

Managed solutions A half-way house between bespoke and outsourced solutions, this involves renting a customised suite of CRM applications as a bespoke package. This can be cost effective but it may mean that you have to compromise in terms of functionality.

7.10.3 Business benefits of CRM

Implementing a customer relationship management (CRM) solution might involve considerable time and expense. However, there are many potential benefits.

A major benefit can be the development of better relations with your existing customers, which can lead to;

- Increased sales through better timing by anticipating needs based on historic trends
- Identifying needs more effectively by understanding specific customer requirements
- Cross-selling of other products by highlighting and suggesting alternatives or enhancements
- Identifying which of your customers are profitable and which are not
- This can lead to better marketing of your products or services by focusing on:
- Effective targeted marketing communications aimed specifically at customer needs
- A more personal approach and the development of new or improved products and services in order to win more business in the future
- Ultimately this could lead to:
- Enhanced customer satisfaction and retention, ensuring that your good reputation in the marketplace continues to grow
- Increased value from your existing customers and reduced costs associated with supporting and servicing them, increasing your overall efficiency and reducing total cost of sales
- Improved profitability by focusing on the most profitable customers and dealing with the unprofitable in more cost effective ways

Once your business starts to look after its existing customers effectively, efforts can be concentrated on finding new customers and expanding your market. The more you know about your customers, the easier it is to identify new prospects and increase your customer base.

Even with years of accumulated knowledge, there is always room for improvement. Customer needs change over time, and technology can make it easier to find out more about customers and ensure that everyone in an organisation can exploit this information.

CHAPTER EIGHT

DATA PROTECTION LEGISLATION

Introduction

Data protection laws affect how businesses and other organisations are allowed to make use of personal information. You must follow these rules if your business stores or processes people's details - ie keeps customer or employee records.

This guide explains the requirements of the Data Protection Act 1998 and outlines steps you can take to ensure you meet them. This may involve notifying the Information Commissioner's Office (ICO) about what personal information your business holds and what it's used for.

You will find specific guidance on what you should consider when recruiting staff and managing employee records, as well the rules on monitoring workers. This guide also contains advice on training your staff to ensure they understand the implications of the Act.

8.1 What does the Data Protection Act 1998 apply to?

The Data Protection Act 1998 applies to personal information. This is data about living, identified, or identifiable individuals and includes information such as names and addresses, bank details, and opinions expressed about an individual.

8.2 What are the main requirements?

The Act regulates how personal information is used, and requires organisations to comply with eight principles - or rules - of good information handling. It also requires some organisations to tell the ICO what they use personal information for.

The Data Protection Act 1998 governs the use of personal information through the eight data protection principles.

These principles require that personal information is:
- Processed fairly and lawfully
- Processed for limited purposes
- Adequate, relevant and not excessive
- Accurate and up to date
- Not kept for longer than is necessary
- Processed in line with the rights of individuals secure
- Not transferred to other countries without adequate protection

The definition of processing is wide and covers virtually any action carried out on a computer. This includes obtaining, recording, holding, processing, and analysing personal information.

If you are processing personal information covered by the Act, you and your staff must comply with the data protection principles. Complying with the principles is largely a matter of common sense and you may well be meeting the requirements already. However, if you need advice on what is required, you can contact the ICO Helpline on Tel 0303 123 1113.

8.3 Data security

Your business must have appropriate security measures in place to protect personal information against unlawful or unauthorised use or disclosure.

Personal information can be used by an organisation only where it meets one of six conditions set out in the Act. In most cases, it should not be too difficult to meet one of these conditions - which include having the individual's consent or having a legitimate interest in using their personal information.

8.4 Sensitive personal data

The Act classifies some personal information as 'sensitive' and there are stricter rules about this type of data. This is information about;

- Racial or ethnic origin
- Political opinions
- Religious or similar beliefs
- Trade union membership
- Physical or mental health condition sexual life offences or alleged offences committed
- Proceedings relating to those offences or alleged offences

You can only use sensitive personal information where you can meet at least one of a narrower set of conditions - as well as being able to meet one of the six standard conditions - for processing personal information. These narrower conditions make sure that this sensitive information is only used where there is an essential need for an organisation to use it.

The first data protection principle requires, among other things, that you must be able to satisfy one or more "conditions for processing" in relation to your processing of personal data. Many (but not all) of these conditions relate to the purpose or purposes for which you intend to use the information.

The conditions for processing take account of the nature of the personal data in question. The conditions that need to be met are more exacting when the information being processed is sensitive personal data, such as information about an individual's health or criminal record.

However, our view is that in determining if you have a legitimate reason for processing personal data, the best approach is to focus on whether what you intend to do is fair. If it is, then you are very likely to identify a condition for processing that fits your purpose.

Being able to satisfy a condition for processing will not on its own guarantee that the processing is fair and lawful – fairness and legality must still be looked at separately. So it makes sense to ensure that what you want to do with personal data is fair and lawful before worrying about the conditions for processing set out in the Act.

8.5 What are the conditions for processing?

The conditions for processing are set out in Schedules 2 and 3 to the Data Protection Act. Unless a relevant exemption applies, at least one of the following conditions must be met whenever you process personal data;

- The individual who the personal data is about has consented to the processing.
- The processing is necessary;
  - in relation to a contract which the individual has entered into; or
  - because the individual has asked for something to be done so they can enter into a contract.
- The processing is necessary because of a legal obligation that applies to you (except an obligation imposed by a contract).
- The processing is necessary to protect the individual's "vital interests". This condition only applies in cases of life or death, such as where an individual's medical history is disclosed to a hospital's A&E department treating them after a serious road accident.
- The processing is necessary for administering justice, or for exercising statutory, governmental, or other public functions.

- The processing is in accordance with the "legitimate interests" condition.

8.6 What is the "legitimate interests" condition?

The Data Protection Act recognises that you may have legitimate reasons for processing personal data that the other conditions for processing do not specifically deal with. The "legitimate interests" condition is intended to permit such processing, provided you meet certain requirements.

The first requirement is that you must need to process the information for the purposes of your legitimate interests or for those of a third party to whom you disclose it.

8.7 Conditions needed in respect of sensitive personal data

At least one of the conditions must be met whenever you process personal data. However, if the information is sensitive personal data, at least one of several other conditions must also be met before the processing can comply with the first data protection principle. These other conditions are as follows;

- The individual who the sensitive personal data is about has given explicit consent to the processing.
- The processing is necessary so that you can comply with employment law.
- The processing is necessary to protect the vital interests of;
  - the individual (in a case where the individual's consent cannot be given or reasonably obtained), or
  - another person (in a case where the individual's consent has been unreasonably withheld)

- The processing is carried out by a not-for-profit organisation and does not involve disclosing personal data to a third party, unless the individual consents. Extra limitations apply to this condition.
- The individual has deliberately made the information public.
- The processing is necessary in relation to legal proceedings; for obtaining legal advice; or otherwise for establishing, exercising, or defending legal rights.
- The processing is necessary for administering justice, or for exercising statutory or governmental functions.
- The processing is necessary for medical purposes, and is undertaken by a health professional or by someone who is subject to an equivalent duty of confidentiality.
- The processing is necessary for monitoring equality of opportunity, and is carried out with appropriate safeguards for the rights of individuals.

In addition to the above conditions – which are all set out in the Data Protection Act itself – regulations set out several other conditions for processing sensitive personal data. Their effect is to permit the processing of sensitive personal data for a range of other purposes – typically those that are in the substantial public interest, and which must necessarily be carried out without the explicit consent of the individual. Examples of such purposes include preventing or detecting crime and protecting the public against malpractice or maladministration.

8.8 When is processing 'necessary'?

Many of the conditions for processing depend on the processing being 'necessary' for the particular purpose to which the condition relates. This imposes a strict requirement, because the condition will not be met if the organisation can achieve the purpose by some other reasonable means or if the processing is necessary only because the organisation has decided to operate its business in a particular way.

8.9 The Data Protection Act distinguishes between;

- The nature of the consent required to satisfy the first condition for processing; and
- The nature of the consent required to satisfy the condition for processing sensitive personal data, which must be 'explicit'.

This suggests that the individual's consent should be clear. It should cover the specific processing details; the type of information (or even the specific information); the purposes of the processing; and any special aspects that may affect the individual, such as any disclosures that may be made.

As explained above, a particular consent may not be adequate to satisfy the condition for processing (especially if the individual might have had no real choice about giving it), and even a valid consent may be withdrawn in some circumstances.

For these reasons an organisation should not rely exclusively on consent to legitimise its processing. In our view it is better to concentrate on making sure that you treat individuals fairly rather than on obtaining consent in isolation. Consent is the first in the list of conditions for processing set out in the Act, but each condition provides an equally valid basis for processing personal data.

CHAPTER NINE

Increase Your Sales

Introduction

The techniques and methods used for research have evolved over the years as different methods of communication and data collection have emerged and statistical tools have been developed.

These require a level of technical understanding to use them to their full potential and enable information to be obtained and extracted from the data to really help the decision process.

9.1 Get old customers back

If people have bought from you before, they may buy from you again. You need to find out why they stopped buying from you and apply that knowledge to regain their custom.

9.2 Find out what changed

Identify why customers stopped buying from you. Consider whether your product or service is;

- No longer necessary
- Too expensive
- Unsatisfactory
- Being beaten by a competitive offer

9.3 Rebuild contact with your customers

Research suggests the reason many customers stop buying is because they don't feel that they have sufficient contact with their suppliers.

Try to have some form of regular contact - eg monthly or quarterly phone calls, formal or informal visits to customers, mail shots, or email newsletters - so that customers do not feel they are being ignored and look elsewhere.

If you have lost a customer for this reason, your first step is to rebuild contact and prove that you understand and are focused on their needs - eg a letter expressing regret that they have stopped buying from you and making them a time-limited offer.

It's worth trying a few times, but don't persist if you aren't getting any response. Many businesses have a limit to the amount of times they contact lapsed customers - usually five or seven times.

9.4 Make an offer to tempt them back

When you know why the customer is no longer buying from you, consider ways to make your business more appealing.

For example, if your price was viewed as too high, consider a time-limited discount to encourage them to start buying again, eg 20 per cent off for three months.

If your service was unsatisfactory, ask what you could do to make it meet your customer's expectations and assess if it is possible and profitable for you to adapt your service for the former customer.

9.5 Be realistic

While you may be able to tempt many customers back, remember that you don't want them at all costs. You want to build a long-term profitable relationship.

It's not usually a good idea to make long-term offers that don't contribute any profit just to get a specific customer back, unless there are compelling strategic reasons to do so.

All these actions should be built into your marketing plan. The faster you contact a lapsed customer, the greater the chance they will come back to you.

- Use information about your competitors to take advantage of any gaps in the market
- Protect your intellectual property, eg the name of your business, your brand, the products or services you make or provide, or the written or artistic material you create
- Improve your ability to tender for contracts
- Design and develop new products or services
- Improve the technology your business uses
- Source your supplies strategically
- Form partnerships with other businesses
- Export your products or services
- Do more business with or in mainland Europe
- Conduct staff training and professional development

9.6 Competing in markets dominated by big brands

What big businesses say about small businesses; Knowing what larger businesses say about working with smaller organizations gives an insight into opportunities to maximize and traps to avoid.

9.6.1 What big businesses appreciate about smaller businesses

- They take greater care with the details
- They offer a more personal service
- The personal chemistry between individuals doing business is better
- What big businesses dislike about smaller businesses
- They are less competitive price-wise
- Their approach is less professional
- They offer less support, such as 24-hour back-up
- Larger businesses clearly value the friendliness and personal approach of the smaller organisation. However, when they are buying goods or services from you, their business decisions are going to be made on more than this
- Small businesses have two big advantages that their bigger competitors lack - agility and flexibility. The successful proposition to a large customer will exploit these advantages to the full

9.7 Growing relationships with big business

Winning business from large companies is an investment in time and effort. Once that business is won, it makes sense to nurture the relationship to ensure it thrives and grows.

Keep in touch-Once you have established a good relationship with the client, stay in touch. Keep aware of changes in their business and how they affect you. Ensure that they can always contact someone in your business who knows about their business. Personally introduce a trusted colleague to the client as back up if you are unavailable.

Update your knowledge- Keep your research up to date - make sure you know how the customer's business sector is changing and developing, and what your competitors are doing. Look out for new opportunities, and discuss them with the client.

Protect your interests - Take care of your property - hopefully your contacts are trustworthy, but keep aware. Protect your intellectual property and take legal advice on contracts. Ask for confidentiality from clients when appropriate. A reputable business will see this as professional and right. Don't give your business away.

Be flexible but sensible- Be flexible, but beware of offering things you can't deliver. Getting and keeping the business is very important, but don't appear to resort to desperate measures. Be prepared to walk away from a contract that stretches your resources too far, or is too tentative - it is not worth putting your business at risk for a single client - at any price.

Keep your business balanced- A huge contract with a single big customer can be a threat to your business rather than an opportunity. Aim to spread the load between several larger clients, and don't neglect your smaller clients for the big ones. Remember that another way to work with big business is to work with the smaller ones as they grow.

9.8 Offering social and ethical incentives

The growing market for 'ethical' products, services, and enterprises could give smaller businesses the opportunity to thrive.

By offering social or ethical incentives that are either not available to the big players or that they would find difficult to sustain, smaller businesses can make an impact on big-brand dominated markets. Smaller providers can bring these incentives to market before the larger competitors and would be able to maintain them for longer.

Customers look more and more for **ethical alternatives** when they buy, and the customer base that makes such a choice is a loyal one. The following are all examples of niche markets originally fulfilled solely by smaller concerns;

- Wood from sustainable sources
- Free-range meat
- Organic food and products
- Fair trade
- Products developed without chemicals
- Cosmetics tested without animals
- Clothes produced without child labour
- Low-energy and other products with reduced environmental impacts

It is, however, clear that the big names have been influenced by customer demand to start thinking along ethical lines.

The concept of traded goods has moved on from coffee and tea to encompass a whole range of clothing, household goods and artworks, sold with the guarantee of a fair share of the profits for the **producers**.

Consumers buying locally produced goods - both consumables and otherwise - helps to reduce carbon footprints, as do initiatives to grow and eat foods in natural season.

Social incentives might include support for charities through a proportion of sales or sales of a particular line, willingness to support local initiatives through donation of goods or services, advertising of events and sponsorship. Co-operation with other small businesses in different markets to offer loyalty savings to each other's customers can be a good way to increase custom.

While an incentive itself is unlikely to create the market for a product, it can greatly enhance the selling proposition, and help retain custom for the future.

CHAPTER TEN

HEALTH AND SAFETY REGULATIONS AT WORK

Introduction

These Regulations may be cited as the Health and Safety at Work etc. Act 1974 (Application to Environmentally Hazardous Substances) (Amendment) Regulations 2005 and shall come into force on 3rd June 2005.

10.1 General duties of employers to their employees

(1)It shall be the duty of every employer to ensure, so far as is reasonably practicable, the health, safety and welfare at work of all his employees.

(2)Without prejudice to the generality of an employer's duty under the preceding subsection, the matters to which that duty extends include in particular;

(a)the provision and maintenance of plant and systems of work that are, so far as is reasonably practicable, safe and without risks to health;

(b)arrangements for ensuring, so far as is reasonably practicable, safety and absence of risks to health in connection with the use, handling, storage and transport of articles and substances;

(c)the provision of such information, instruction, training and supervision as is necessary to ensure, so far as is reasonably practicable, the health and safety at work of his employees;

(d)so far as is reasonably practicable as regards any place of work under the employer's control, the maintenance of it in a condition that is safe and without risks to health and the provision and maintenance of means of access to and egress from it that are safe and without such risks;

(e)the provision and maintenance of a working environment for his employees that is, so far as is reasonably practicable, safe, without risks to health, and adequate as regards facilities and arrangements for their welfare at work.

(3)Except in such cases as may be prescribed, it shall be the duty of every employer to prepare and as often as may be appropriate revise a written statement of his general policy with respect to the health and safety at work of his employees and the organisation and arrangements for the time being in force for carrying out that policy, and to bring the statement and any revision of it to the notice of all of his employees.

(4)Regulations made by the Secretary of State may provide for the appointment in prescribed cases by recognised trade unions (within the meaning of the regulations) of safety representatives from amongst the employees, and those representatives shall represent the employees in consultations with the employers under subsection (6) below and shall have such other functions as may be prescribed.

(6)It shall be the duty of every employer to consult any such representatives with a view to the making and maintenance of arrangements which will enable him and his employees to co-operate effectively in promoting and developing measures to ensure the health and safety at work of the employees, and in checking the effectiveness of such measures.

(7)In such cases as may be prescribed it shall be the duty of every employer, if requested to do so by the safety representatives mentioned in above, to establish, in accordance with regulations made by the Secretary of State, a safety committee having the function of keeping under review the measures taken to ensure the health and safety at work of his employees and such other functions as may be prescribed.

10.2 General duties of employers and self-employed to persons other than their employees

(1)It shall be the duty of every employer to conduct his undertaking in such a way as to ensure, so far as is reasonably practicable, that persons not in his employment who may be affected thereby are not thereby exposed to risks to their health or safety.

(2)It shall be the duty of every self-employed person to conduct his undertaking in such a way as to ensure, so far as is reasonably practicable, that he and other persons (not being his employees) who may be affected thereby are not thereby exposed to risks to their health or safety.

(3)In such cases as may be prescribed, it shall be the duty of every employer and every self-employed person, in the prescribed circumstances and in the prescribed manner, to give to persons (not being his employees) who may be affected by the way in which he conducts his undertaking the prescribed information about such aspects of the way in which he conducts his undertaking as might affect their health or safety.

10.3 General duties of persons concerned with premises to persons other than their employees.

(1)This section has effect for imposing on persons duties in relation to those who;

(a)are not their employees; but

(b)use non-domestic premises made available to them as a place of work or as a place where they may use plant or substances provided for their use there,and applies to premises so made available and other non-domestic premises used in connection with them.

(2)It shall be the duty of each person who has, to any extent, control of premises to which this section applies or of the means of access there to or egress there from or of any plant or substance in such premises to take such measures as it is reasonable for a person in his position to take to ensure, so far as is reasonably practicable, that the premises, all means of access thereto or egress therefrom available for use by persons using the premises, and any plant or substance in the premises or, as the case may be, provided for use there, is or are safe and without risks to health.

(3)Where a person has, by virtue of any contract or tenancy, an obligation of any extent in relation to;

(a) the maintenance or repair of any premises to which this section applies or any means of access thereto or egress therefrom; or

(b) the safety of or the absence of risks to health arising from plant or substances in any such premises; that person shall be treated, for the purposes of subsection (2) above, as being a person who has control of the matters to which his obligation extends.

(4) Any reference in this section to a person having control of any premises or matter is a reference to a person having control of the premises or matter in connection with the carrying on by him of a trade, business or other undertaking (whether for profit or not).

10.4 General duty of persons in control of certain premises in relation to harmful emissions into atmosphere

(1) subject to subsection (5) below,] It shall be the duty of the person having control of any premises of a class prescribed for the purposes of section 1(1)(d) to use the best practicable means for preventing the emission into the atmosphere from the premises of noxious or offensive substances and for rendering harmless and inoffensive such substances as may be so emitted.

(2) The reference in subsection (1) above to the means to be used for the purposes there mentioned includes a reference to the manner in which the plant provided for those purposes is used and to the supervision of any operation involving the emission of the substances to which that subsection applies.

(3) Any substance or a substance of any description prescribed for the purposes of subsection (1) above as noxious or offensive shall be a noxious or, as the case may be, an offensive substance for those purposes whether or not it would be so apart from this subsection.

(4) Any reference in this section to a person having control of any premises is a reference to a person having control of the premises in connection with the carrying on by him of a trade, business or other

undertaking (whether for profit or not) and any duty imposed on any such person by this section shall extend only to matters within his control.

(5) The foregoing provisions of this section shall not apply in relation to any process which is a prescribed process as from the date which is the determination date for that process.

(6) For the purposes of subsection (5) above, the "determination date" for a prescribed process is;

(a) in the case of a process for which an authorisation is granted, the date on which the enforcing authority grants it, whether in pursuance of the application or, on an appeal, of a direction to grant it;

(b) in the case of a process for which an authorisation is refused, the date of the refusal or, on an appeal, of the affirmation of the refusal.

(7) In subsections (5) and (6) above "authorisation", "enforcing authority" and "prescribed process" have the meaning given in section 1 of the Environmental Protection Act 1990 and the reference to an appeal is a reference to an appeal under section 15 of that Act.]]

10.5 General duties of manufacturers etc. as regards articles and substances for use at work

(1) It shall be the duty of any person who designs, manufactures, imports or supplies any article for use at work or any article of fairground equipment.

(a) to ensure, so far as is reasonably practicable, that the article is so designed and constructed that it will be safe and without risks to health at all times when it is being set, used, cleaned or maintained by a person at work;

(b) to carry out or arrange for the carrying out of such testing and examination as may be necessary for the performance of the duty imposed on him by the preceding paragraph;

(c) to take such steps as are necessary to secure that persons supplied by that person with the article are provided with adequate information about the use for which the article is designed or has been tested and about any conditions necessary to ensure that it will be safe and without risks to health at all such times as are mentioned in paragraph (a) above and when it is being dismantled or disposed of; and

(d)to take such steps as are necessary to secure, so far as is reasonably practicable, that persons so supplied are provided with all such revisions of information provided to them by virtue of the preceding paragraph as are necessary by reason of its becoming known that anything gives rise to a serious risk to health or safety.

(1A)It shall be the duty of any person who designs, manufactures, imports or supplies any article of fairground equipment;

(a)to ensure, so far as is reasonably practicable, that the article is so designed and constructed that it will be safe and without risks to health at all times when it is being used for or in connection with the entertainment of members of the public;

(b)to carry out or arrange for the carrying out of such testing and examination as may be necessary for the performance of the duty imposed on him by the preceding paragraph;

(c)to take such steps as are necessary to secure that persons supplied by that person with the article are provided with adequate information about the use for which the article is designed or has been tested and about any conditions necessary to ensure that it will be safe and without risks to health at all times when it is being used for or in connection with the entertainment of members of the public; and

(d)to take such steps as are necessary to secure, so far as is reasonably practicable, that persons so supplied are provided with all such revisions of information provided to them by virtue of the preceding paragraph as are necessary by reason of its becoming known that anything gives rise to a serious risk to health or safety.

(2)It shall be the duty of any person who undertakes the design or manufacture of any article for use at work or of any article of fairground equipment] to carry out or arrange for the carrying out of any necessary research with a view to the discovery and, so far as is reasonably practicable, the elimination or minimisation of any risks to health or safety to which the design or article may give rise.

(3)It shall be the duty of any person who erects or installs any article for use at work in any premises where that article is to be used by persons at work or who erects or installs any article of fairground equipment] to ensure, so far as is reasonably practicable, that nothing about the way in which the article is erected or installed makes it unsafe or a risk to health at any such time as is mentioned in paragraph (a) of subsection (1) or, as the case may be, in paragraph (a) of subsection (1) or (1A) above.]

(4)It shall be the duty of any person who manufactures, imports or supplies any substance;

(a)to ensure, so far as is reasonably practicable, that the substance will be safe and without risks to health at all times when it is being used, handled, processed, stored or transported by a person at work or in premises to which section 4 above applies;

(b)to carry out or arrange for the carrying out of such testing and examination as may be necessary for the performance of the duty imposed on him by the preceding paragraph

(c)to take such steps as are necessary to secure that persons supplied by that person with the substance are provided with adequate information about any risks to health or safety to which the inherent properties of the substance may give rise, about the results of any relevant tests which have been carried out on or in connection with the substance and about any conditions necessary to ensure that the substance will be safe and without risks to health at all such times as are mentioned in paragraph (a) above and when the substance is being disposed of; and

(d)to take such steps as are necessary to secure, so far as is reasonably practicable, that persons so supplied are provided with all such revisions of information provided to them by virtue of the preceding paragraph as are necessary by reason of its becoming known that anything gives rise to a serious risk to health or safety.

(5)It shall be the duty of any person who undertakes the manufacture of any substance to carry out or arrange for the carrying out of any necessary research with a view to the discovery and, so far as is reasonable practicable, the elimination or minimisation of any risks to health or safety to which the substance may give rise at all such times as are mentioned in paragraph (a) of subsection (4) above].

(6)Nothing in the preceding provisions of this section shall be taken to require a person to repeat any testing, examination or research which has been carried out otherwise than by him or at his instance, in so far as it is reasonable for him to rely on the results thereof for the purposes of those provisions.

(7)Any duty imposed on any person by any of the preceding provisions of this section shall extend only to things done in the course of a trade, business or other undertaking carried on by him (whether for profit or not) and to matters within his control.

(8)Where a person designs, manufactures, imports or supplies an article for use at work or an article of fairground equipment and does so for or to another] on the basis of a written undertaking by that other to take specified steps sufficient to ensure, so far as is reasonably practicable, that the article will be safe and without risks to health at all such times as are mentioned in paragraph (a) of subsection (1) or, as the case may be, in paragraph (a) of subsection (1) or (1A) above], the undertaking shall have the effect of relieving the first-mentioned person from the duty imposed by virtue of that paragraph] to such extent as is reasonable having regard to the terms of the undertaking.

(8A)Nothing in subsection (7) or (8) above shall relieve any person who imports any article or substance from any duty in respect of anything which;

(a)in the case of an article designed outside the United Kingdom, was done by and in the course of any trade, profession or other undertaking carried on by, or was within the control of, the person who designed the article; or

(b)in the case of an article or substance manufactured outside the United Kingdom, was done by and in the course of any trade, profession or other undertaking carried on by, or was within the control of, the person who manufactured the article or substance.

(9)Where a person ("the ostensible supplier") supplies any article or substance] to another ("the customer") under a hire-purchase agreement, conditional sale agreement or credit-sale agreement, and the ostensible supplier;

(a)carries on the business of financing the acquisition of goods by others by means of such agreements; and

(b)in the course of that business acquired his interest in the article or substance supplied to the customer as a means of financing its acquisition by the customer from a third person ("the effective supplier"), the effective supplier and not the ostensible supplier shall be treated for the purposes of this section as supplying the article or substance to the customer, and any duty imposed by the preceding provisions of this section on suppliers shall accordingly fall on the effective supplier and not on the ostensible supplier.

(10)For the purposes of this section an absence of safety or a risk to health shall be disregarded in so far as the case in or in relation to which it would arise is shown to be one the occurrence of which could not reasonably be foreseen; and in determining whether any duty imposed by virtue of paragraph (a) of subsection (1), (1A) or (4) above has been performed regard shall be had to any relevant information or advice which has been provided to any person by the person by whom the article has been designed, manufactured, imported or supplied or, as the case may be, by the person by whom the substance has been manufactured, imported or supplied.

10.6 General duties of employees at work

It shall be the duty of every employee while at work;

(a)to take reasonable care for the health and safety of himself and of other persons who may be affected by his acts or omissions at work; and

(b)as regards any duty or requirement imposed on his employer or any other person by or under any of the relevant statutory provisions, to co-operate with him so far as is necessary to enable that duty or requirement to be performed or complied with.

10.7 Duty not to interfere with or misuse things provided pursuant to certain provisions.

No person shall intentionally or recklessly interfere with or misuse anything provided in the interests of health, safety, or welfare in pursuance of any of the relevant statutory provisions.

10.8 Duty not to charge employees for things done or provided pursuant to certain specific requirements.

No employer shall levy or permit to be levied on any employee of his any charge in respect of anything done or provided in pursuance of any specific requirement of the relevant statutory provisions.

For more information please visit the web; www.legislation.gov.uk

CHAPTER ELEVEN

WHOLESALE SUPPLIERS

11.1 Business to Business Directory In England

www.Applegate.co.uk - For over 14 years The Applegate Directory has continued to be the UK's largest, most comprehensive and widely used directory for industry, manufacturing and technology companies in England and rest of the UK.

Applegate is used by key decision makers across all industry sectors. Being online has the benefit of a fast and effective form of advertising and is available anytime day or night.

www.applegate.co.uk

Product Range

- Aerospace
- Business Services
- Chemical, Oil & Gas
- Construction
- Electronics
- Engineering
- Food & Agribusiness
- IT for Industry
- Packaging & Transport
- Pharmaceuticals

- Plastics & Rubber
- Recruitment Services
- Renewables
- Textiles & Clothing

Applegate Directory Ltd

Riverside Road,Pottington Business Park

Barnstaple Devon, EX31 1LS (Road Map)

Tel: 01271 852000

Fax: 01271 376386

Number of Employees: 21 - 100

www.applegate.co.uk

marketing@applegate.co.uk

11.2 Business to Business Directory outside England

www.Alibaba.com (HKSE: 1688) (1688.HK) is the global leader in e-commerce for small businesses and the flagship company of Alibaba Group.

Founded in 1999 in Hangzhou, China, Alibaba.com makes it easy for millions of buyers and suppliers around the world to do business online mainly through three marketplaces: a global trade platform (www.alibaba.com) for importers and exporters; a Chinese platform (www.1688.com) for domestic trade in China; and a transaction-based wholesale platform on the global site (www.aliexpress.com) geared for smaller buyers seeking fast shipment of small quantities of goods. Together, these marketplaces form a community of close to 72.8 million registered users in more than 240 countries and regions.

As part of its strategy to transition into a holistic platform where small companies can build and manage their online business more easily,

Alibaba.com also offers Chinese traders a wide array of business management software, Internet infrastructure services and export-related services directly or through companies it has acquired including HiChina and One-Touch, as well as educational services to incubate enterprise management and e-commerce professionals. Alibaba.com also owns Vendio and Auctiva, leading providers of third-party e-commerce solutions for online merchants.

Alibaba.com has offices in more than 70 cities across Greater China, India, Japan, Korea, Europe and the United States

www.alibaba.com

Product Range

- Agriculture
  rice, cigarettes, apples
- Apparel
  hair band, hair wigs, silk tie
- Automobiles & Motorcycles
  car dvd player, atv, car gps
- Beauty & Personal Care
  baby clothing, bathing suits, bras
- Business Services
  advertising, bathing suits, consulting
- Chemicals
  antivirus, painting, adhesives
- Computer Hardware & Software
  laptop, usb flash drive, software
- Construction & Real Estate
  marble, granite, flooring

- Consumer Electronics
  mp3 player, mp4 player, lcd tv
- Electrical Equipment & Supplies
  batteries, connectors, generators
- Electronic Components & Supplies
  led displays, led signs, lcd panels
- Energy
  biodiesel, bitumen, charcoal
- Environment
  gas disposal, recycled plastic, recycling
- Excess Inventory
  apparel stock, gifts & crafts stocks, home supplies stocks
- Fashion Accessories
  hair band, hair wigs, silk tie
- Food & Beverage
  sugar, chocolate, wine
- Furniture
  sofa, chair, bed
- General Industrial Equipment
  engines, air compressor, welding machine
- Gifts & Crafts
  candle, wooden box, wedding gifts
- Hardware
  anchors, bolts, brackets
- Health & Medical
  sex products, condom, herb medicine Home & Garden
  tableware, storage box, umbrella
- Home Appliances
  solar air conditioner, solar water heater, ceiling fan
- Lights & Lighting
  chandelier,energy saving, flashlights

- Luggage, Bags & Cases
  handbag, wallet, bag
- Manufacturing & Processing Machinery
  used machine, printing machine, packing machine
- Measurement & Analysis Instruments
  analyzers , counters , multimeters
- Mechanical Parts & Fabrication Services
  bamboos floor, ceramics tiles, doors
- Minerals & Metallurgy
  steel pipe, stainless steel, casting
- Office & School Supplies
  a4 paper, ball pen, calculator
- Packaging & Printing
  gift box, plastic bag, paper bag
- Rubber & Plastics
  abs, epdm, hdpe
- Security & Protection
  access control card, alcohol tester, cctv camera
- Service Equipment
  advertising equipment, advertising screens , advertising light boxes
- Shoes & Accessories
  women's-shoe, slipper, sandals
- Sport & Entertainment
  segway, scooter, pocket bike
- Telecommunications
  rotatable cell phone, watch phone, transparent phone
- Textiles & Leather Products
  fabric, cotton fabric, yarn
- Timepieces, Jewelry & Eyewear
  jewelry, watch, eyewear

- Tools
  power tools, cordless tools, air pump
- Toys & Hobbies
  rc helicopter, dolls, rc car
- Transportation
  bicycle, bicycle frame, bus